Bad to the Bone
NASTIEST ANIMALS

Mongooses

By John O'Mara

 Gareth Stevens
PUBLISHING

Please visit our website, www.garethstevens.com. For a free color catalog of all our high-quality books, call toll free 1-800-542-2595 or fax 1-877-542-2596.

Library of Congress Cataloging-in-Publication Data

O'Mara, John, author.
 Mongooses / John O'Mara.
     pages cm. — (Bad to the bone. Nastiest animals)
 Includes bibliographical references and index.
 ISBN 978-1-4824-1962-7 (pbk.)
 ISBN 978-1-4824-1961-0 (6 pack)
 ISBN 978-1-4824-1963-4 (library binding)
 1. Mongooses—Juvenile literature. I. Title.
 QL737.C235O43 2015
 599.74'2—dc23

                                    2014025643

First Edition

Published in 2015 by
Gareth Stevens Publishing
111 East 14th Street, Suite 349
New York, NY 10003

Copyright © 2015 Gareth Stevens Publishing

Designer: Michael Flynn
Editor: Therese Shea

Photo credits: Cover, p. 1 Pal Teravagimov/Shutterstock.com; cover, pp. 1–24 (series art) foxie/Shutterstock.com; cover, pp. 1–24 (series art) Larysa Ray/Shutterstock.com; cover, pp. 1–24 (series art) LeksusTuss/Shutterstock.com; p. 5 Dorling Kindersley/Getty Images; p. 7 Nelson Marques/Shutterstock.com; p. 9 (Egyptian mongoose) Suzi Eszterhas/Minden Pictures/Getty Images; p. 9 (dwarf mongoose) © iStockphoto.com/BigdogKen; p. 9 (Indian gray mongoose) David Courtenay/Oxford Scientific/Getty Images; p. 11 Alex Bowie/Hulton Archive/Getty Images; p. 13 © iStockphoto.com/Mendelewski; p. 15 Mark Deeble and Victoria Stone/Photodisc/Getty Images; p. 17 Villiers Steyn/Shutterstock.com; p. 19 Ann and Steve Toon/Robert Harding World Imagery/Getty Images; p. 21 Chris Johns/National Geographic/Getty Images.

Printed in the United States of America

CPSIA compliance information: Batch #CW15GS: For further information contact Gareth Stevens, New York, New York at 1-800-542-2595.

Contents

Words in the glossary appear in **bold** type the first time they are used in the text.

Mad, Bad Mongooses

With their long body, short legs, and pointy **snouts**, mongooses are cute, furry animals—unless you're an enemy. Then, it doesn't matter how dangerous you are—they aren't afraid to fight.

Mongooses are famous for taking on and killing **venomous** snakes such as king cobras and adders. Are these little creatures crazy? No, they just know they're tough enough to win a fight. How can this be? These tricky animals have **adaptations** that help keep them alive.

That's Nasty!

Mongoose mummies have been found in Egypt!

Mongooses have claws that are always out.

Mongooses on the Map

Mongooses are mostly found in Africa. However, some live in southern Asia and southern Europe. Mongooses are mostly land animals, but a few kinds spend time in water, while others hang out in trees.

Mongooses can live in many kinds of **habitats**. They're found in deserts, forests, and grasslands. They live anywhere they can find a lot of food.

Some kinds of mongooses like to live alone their whole life. Others live in colonies of more than 50 mongooses!

Europe

Asia

Africa

Indian
Ocean

Australia

mongoose habitats

This map shows the parts of Africa, Asia, and
Europe where mongooses can be found.

7

Many Mongooses

There are about 34 species, or kinds, of mongooses. The biggest mongooses, Egyptian mongooses, are 25 inches (64 cm) long and weigh 11 pounds (5 kg). The smallest, the dwarf mongooses, are 7 inches (18 cm) long and weigh 12 ounces (340 g). In addition, a mongoose's tail can be up to 21 inches (53 cm) long.

One of the most famous species is the Indian gray mongoose. That's because a famous author, Rudyard Kipling, wrote a story about a **fictional** one called Rikki-tikki-tavi.

That's Nasty!

Mongooses have 35 to 40 sharp teeth.

dwarf mongoose

Egyptian mongoose

Indian gray mongoose

Mongooses can be different colors, but most are brown or gray. Some are striped.

Mongoose vs. Cobra

The king cobra doesn't have the most poisonous snake venom. However, it delivers a lot of it into its enemies through its 1/2-inch (1.3 cm) fangs. Its bite is enough to kill a small animal like a mongoose quickly.

The mongoose has excellent **reflexes**, though. It can move quickly out of the way as a cobra is about to strike. The mongoose's strong jaws and sharp bites can really hurt a cobra. A mongoose can crack the snake's skull! Usually, the mongoose repeatedly attacks until the snake is dead.

That's Nasty!

A king cobra bite can kill a human in 15 minutes and an elephant in a few hours.

The mongoose is about to strike—before the cobra does!

11

Stronger Than Venom?

Sometimes a mongoose isn't fast enough to escape a cobra's poisonous bite. Mongooses often manage to survive these venomous attacks, though. How do they do this?

Scientists think mongooses have passed down a **resistance** to the poison over time. Their **ancestors** were probably bitten many times, and the animals that survived the bites passed on their resistance to their children. However, if mongooses are attacked enough and take too much venom into their body, they still die.

That's Nasty!

One fight between a mongoose and a cobra was reported to have lasted for more than 1 hour.

A mongoose's thick coat may also help protect it from venomous bites.

Mongoose Meals

What does a mongoose do after defeating a cobra? It eats it! Mongooses are carnivores, or meat eaters. They eat **rodents**, birds, **reptiles**, and eggs. Some eat plants and fruits. Mongooses that spend time in water eat fish and crabs. A few species are great at catching flying bugs.

Some mongooses have been seen opening eggs in an interesting way. They carry the egg to a rock, turn around on their back legs, and throw the egg through their legs behind them. They do this until the eggshell breaks.

That's Nasty!

Some mongoose species also eat carrion—dead animals.

This mongoose is eating a baby crocodile
right out of an egg.

15

Packed Burrows

Most mongooses live in **burrows** that cover a large area. Usually, they dig them with their sharp claws. However, they may use an empty burrow that another animal has already dug. Most species of mongooses are active during the day. They're sometimes seen standing on their back legs, looking out for predators, such as **birds of prey**.

Mongooses that live in packs, such as Ethiopian dwarf mongooses, hunt in large groups. This means they can overpower big prey by all attacking at once.

That's Nasty!

Some mongooses puff out their fur to look bigger to their enemies.

These dwarf mongooses keep watch outside
their burrow. If they see a snake or bird,
they make a call to others in the pack.

Mongoose Pups

Mother mongooses give birth to pups four times a year. All the mothers in a pack give birth on the same day! The whole pack takes care of feeding the pups, who stay in the safety of the burrow for several weeks. Male mongooses stand guard over the burrows.

Pups begin to learn to hunt at around 1 month old. Both mothers and males show them how to find food. The pups are fully grown by the time they're 6 months old.

Male mongooses will leave their mother at around 6 months old. However, female mongooses stay longer or even for the rest of their life.

Introducing the Mongoose

In the 1800s, mongooses were brought to Hawaii and certain islands in the Caribbean Sea. People wanted them to eat the rodents that were eating valuable crops there. While mongooses did this, they also ate other **native** species. They're responsible for some species completely disappearing off the islands.

These hunters are very good at what they do, whether they're stealing eggs out of a bird's nest or fighting a deadly snake. Mongooses are truly one of nature's nastiest animals!

fast reflexes

sharp claws

sharp teeth

Mongooses: So Nasty!

resistant to venom

powerful jaws

A mongoose finds a tasty snack.

Glossary

adaptation: a change in a type of animal that makes it better able to live in its surroundings

ancestor: an animal that lived before others in its family tree

bird of prey: a bird that kills other animals for food and has excellent eyesight, sharp claws, and a sharp beak, such as an owl or hawk

burrow: a hole made by an animal in which it lives or hides

fictional: not real or true

habitat: the natural place where an animal or plant lives

native: grown, produced, or coming from a certain place

reflex: the ability to react quickly

reptile: an animal covered with scales or plates that breathes air, has a backbone, and lays eggs, such as a turtle, snake, lizard, or crocodile

resistance: the ability to remain unchanged by the harmful effect of something

rodent: a small, furry animal with large front teeth, such as a mouse or rat

snout: an animal's nose and mouth

venomous: able to produce a liquid called venom that is harmful to other animals

For More Information

Books

Borgert-Spaniol, Megan. *Mongooses*. Minneapolis, MN: Bellwether Media, 2014.

Kipling, Rudyard. *Rikki-tikki-tavi*. Mankato, MN: Creative Education, 1988.

Sebastian, Emily. *Mongooses*. New York, NY: PowerKids Press, 2012.

Websites

Mongoose
animals.nationalgeographic.com/animals/mammals/mongoose/
Check out National Geographic's Fast Facts for mongooses.

Mongooses
animaldiversity.ummz.umich.edu/accounts/Herpestidae/
Read more about mongooses on this University of Michigan site.

Index